DATING

Other titles in this
series include:

DATING

THE
SCHOOL
OF LIFE

Published in 2019 by The School of Life
First published in the USA in 2020
70 Marchmont Street, London WC1N 1AB
Copyright © The School of Life 2019
Printed in Belgium by Graphius

A proportion of this book has appeared online at
www.theschooloflife.com/thebookoflife

Every effort has been made to contact the copyright holders of
the material reproduced in this book. If any have been inadvertently
overlooked, the publisher will be pleased to make restitution at the
earliest opportunity.

The School of Life is a resource for helping us understand ourselves, for
improving our relationships, our careers and our social lives – as well as
for helping us find calm and get more out of our leisure hours. We do
this through creating films, workshops, books and gifts.
www.theschooloflife.com

ISBN 978-1-912891-04-7

10 9 8 7 6 5 4 3 2

Cover image: ClassicStock / Alamy Stock Photo

CONTENTS

A BRIEF HISTORY OF DATING

Our present dating habits can feel like a natural part of existence, but in reality, they've only been around for a very short time and (we predict) won't continue for too much longer in their current form. Dating has a history, which it pays to try to understand as we navigate the ritual's often paradoxical and tumultuous aspects.

We can take a selective look backwards – as well as a peek forwards – at the history and future of dating:

1489, Medina del Campo, Spain

In a treatise signed between England and Spain, the two-year-old Tudor prince Arthur is formally engaged to Catherine of Aragon, who is at that point three years old. It's an extreme example of what is an entirely normal practice all over the world in the premodern era: Relationships are thought of as strategic transactions between families, where the feelings of the couple themselves are of no importance whatsoever. The idea that you might love, let alone be physically attracted to, the person you ended up married to would have been deemed profoundly irresponsible, if not plain peculiar.

1761, Amsterdam, Netherlands

The publication of *Julie*, a novel by the French Romantic philosopher Jean-Jacques Rousseau, becomes the fastest-selling book ever written. The novel tells the story of Julie, a young woman from an aristocratic family who is expected to marry someone of her standing, but, contrary to all the rules, falls in love with her middle-class teacher, Saint-Preux. However, they cannot get married because of the differences in their social status.

Rousseau is on the side of the unhappy couple – and his novel is the first major statement of the idea that relationships should essentially be founded on the feelings that exist between people, and have nothing to do with class, lineage or family concerns. But as yet, Rousseau and his novel see no way of upturning the social order: You still marry who your parents and society tell you to, but now at least, with Rousseau's help, you can feel very sorry that you have to.

1855, Rome, Italy
In the major Italian novel of the 19th century, *I Vicere* by Federico di Roberto, two characters, Lucrezia and

Benedetto, are in love but can't marry because Lucrezia's mother refuses to give her permission on the grounds of social propriety. Crucially, the mother is shown to be old-fashioned and narrow-minded; couples formed by 'reason' are, the novelist suggests, a lot less happy than those guided by instinct. The book works with the growing Romantic assumption that relationships should be based on sentiment and that the best chance of finding someone we can get on well with over a lifetime is not to fixate on what their job is or whether they come from a good family, but whether we experience an overwhelming physical and emotional attraction in their presence. Marriage should be a sanctioned union consecrated by a wondrous feeling.

1892, London, England

The most successful comic play of the year, *Charley's Aunt*, turns on the fact that Charley has invited Kitty to lunch on a date but, at the last minute, learns that his aunt won't be able to join them. This creates a panic because a dating couple should have a chaperone, an older woman whose presence will ensure that nothing very intimate can be said or done. Charley's solution is to get a male friend to put on a dress and impersonate his relative. The comedic atmosphere of the play suggests that the old rules around dating are firmly on their way out and are accepted as having some of the fustiness of a maiden aunt. The audience is meant to agree that dating couples should be left on their own to discover how they feel; there should even be an option for a little kiss at the end if things go swimmingly (as they do for Charley and Kitty).

1914, Eastbourne, England
The young George Orwell gets into trouble at school when he is caught reading *Youth's Encounter* by Compton

Mackenzie, the first novel published in England that describes unsupervised adolescent dating. We're starting to move beyond the odd chaste kiss: Dating starts to be about sex as well.

1960, *Washington DC, USA*

The US Food and Drug Administration approves the first oral female contraceptive pill. The idea that a date can happily and uncomplicatedly lead to sex becomes not only an emotional but now also a practical possibility.

1998, *Los Angeles, USA*

Speed dating is invented and the romantic comedy *You've Got Mail*, the first major film based around online dating, is released. Both encourage the idea that it's important to search very widely before selecting a possible partner. By now, all the elements of modern dating are in place:

firstly, parents have nothing to do with it; secondly, all considerations of money and social status are deemed 'un-Romantic' and unimportant; thirdly, you are meant to be powerfully emotionally drawn to someone in order for a relationship to be deemed legitimate and viable in the long term; fourthly, sex is interpreted as a central part of getting to know someone; and lastly, you're meant to have a lot of dates (and possibly meet quite a few horrors on the way) before finally and happily settling down with that archetypal figure of the modern dating scene: The One.

2009, Brussels, Belgium
The European Union releases a report that reveals that fifty percent of married couples in countries across the union end up divorced after fifteen years. Though entirely ignored by Europe's dating couples, the report quietly raises the question of whether instinct is really

any better as a guide to a good conjugal life than the old parental or societal rules used to be – as well as hinting at how much more miserable we can end up being when the sole justification for relationships is deemed to be the constant happiness of their participants.

Might there be another way to find our partners going forward? Where might dating be headed in the future?

2075, *Singapore*

Artificial intelligence has finally arrived, human nature has at last accurately been understood and dating as we know it dies. For the first time, machines can entirely accurately predict who should belong with whom. Internet dating algorithms, for so long about as faulty as medieval brain surgery, achieve their promise: Machines now swiftly find us the optimal partner for a lifetime together. They know who is available, what our quirks are and who out there can best complement them. All the rigmarole of dating in the Romantic era is done away with. We no longer have to wonder whether we have found the 'right' person; a machine that we trust as much as we now trust doctors tells us when we have located our destiny. We no longer have to rely on chance or random encounters. We no longer have to keep asking our friends and hoping to be introduced. We don't have to listen to our parents, we don't have to take along a maiden aunt and we don't have to pay attention to those equally unreliable entities, our subjective feelings. Couples are not always deliriously happy, but they at least have the satisfaction of knowing that they are with the person they should, all things being equal, be with.

Way back in 1489, there wasn't any choice for Prince Arthur and Catherine of Aragon; now there is no choice either, but in 2075, it is a psychological machine that has determined where necessity lies.

Occasionally, people get a little nostalgic and curious about the old-fashioned, rather haphazard and sometimes thrilling Romantic way of dating. Some of them might dress up and recreate the ritual, like people who nowadays have fun trying out what it was like to row in a longboat or take part in a medieval joust.

All of which should give us a humbling sense of how particular and complicated contemporary dating truly is. We shouldn't blame ourselves if, at the end of yet another barren or ambiguous date, we feel in need of a little guidance.

EXISTENTIALISM AND DATING

Dating brings us close to a particular strand of philosophy that might not, at first glance, seem particularly relevant to our lives: existentialism. Nevertheless, one of the movement's major proponents – Jean-Paul Sartre – developed a set of ideas that help to explain, and give dignity to, the anxiety, excitement and at points vertigo we may experience as we go through the dating process.

A key concept of existentialism was expressed in Sartre's somewhat obscure but useful phrase: 'Being precedes essence'. What Sartre refers to as 'being' are the bits of our life that we are free to choose for ourselves: where we live, what job we do, how we conceive of what happens to us. By the word 'essence' he refers to things that lie outside our command: our biological nature, the flow of history, the large political currents. Which is more influential, 'being' or 'essence'?

What Sartre wished to point out to us, wanting to liberate us from certain rigidities of mind, is that 'being' should, ultimately, be thought of as more important than 'essence'. However much we sometimes like to tell ourselves that things for us have to be the way they are, there are in fact many radically different possible versions of ourselves available to us; we can choose to an extraordinary extent how things might go. But much of the time, Sartre felt, we don't give this open-ended aspect of our identities enough space in our minds. We assert that the way we live is inevitable and fixed, and imply that we have no agency over our stories. But Sartre argues that this is an illusion: The kind of person we are right now developed as a result of all sorts of small and large decisions; it could have been very different, and may be different again in the future according to the way we exercise our will upon the raw material of life.

Surprisingly enough, it is dating that can bring home some of the richness of this existential insight. It is in our dating years that we feel, perhaps more than at any point before or since, how much our future is undefined, how little is preordained, how many options there really are and how dramatically free and fluid things can be.

With each date, we're sketching – even if only very lightly – an alternative possible future. If our date on Wednesday goes well, we could conceivably be looking at (for instance) a life where we have relatives in the highlands of Scotland, where a lot of the people we spend time with are in the technology sector and where we'll probably move country several times; we might in time also have a child called Hamish or Flora. Alternatively, if our date on Friday evening goes very well, we could be edging towards a life where we'll be spending a lot of time in Amsterdam, where we'll get drawn into the world of the theatre, where if we have a child they might be called Maartje or Rem and where we will have a former cycling champion as a grandfather and an Indonesian grandmother.

Once we make our choice, things may well start to seem as if they always had to be, that there was some essence that we were always moving towards, that we had to end up with little Maartje or sweet Flora crawling on the carpet towards us. But in the dating period, we are closer to a grander and more visceral truth: that there is no single script.

Sartre's second big point is that properly recognising our freedom can lead us to a state of huge but inevitable and in a way salutary anxiety (in his native French, *angoisse*). Conscious of our real liberty, we take on board that we have to make decisions, and yet at the same time that we can never have the correct and full information upon which to base them with the sort of perfect wisdom and foresight we desire. We are steering largely blind, forced to make choices that ideally we'd leave to the gods, but that in a secular world we have no option but to take on ourselves. No wonder that anxiety should be the foremost emotion of our godless age.

As we date, we may wonder: Who should we settle

for? For how long do we keep going? How can we tell whether this one or that one is right?

Sartre's answer is that we can never properly know, but that we are never more properly alive and authentic than when we are turning over such enquiries. The fluidity of our destinies is then palpable, with all the strangeness and wonder involved.

But too often the sense of fluidity is lost. We assume that what is had to be and that we have no further choices left open to us.

However, the dating years, properly interpreted, should defy such views. Sartre wished to embolden us for the sort of challenges that they present to us. Dating pushes aside the veil of our normal complacency and reveals the sublime, terrifying and at the same time thrilling uncertainty of existence. We should, while embracing the anxiety-provoking existential challenges before us, feel a little heroic at least.

A great deal of literature on dating focuses on what we should ideally say to those we're attracted to yet whom we encounter – as we often do – without the help of a formal introduction. Should we chance a remark on the weather or ask directions to a bookshop, compliment them on their bag or ask them how their brunch tastes? What unites the varied recommendations is the notion that it is what we say to another person that in the end crucially determines our level of success in the trials of dating.

But in truth, what we would perhaps be wiser to focus on is what we are able to say to ourselves. The so-called chat-up lines we really need to dwell on are not those we address to another person; they are the ones we direct at our own uncertain and under-confident selves, the lines that can best help us to believe that approaching another person can sometimes be a legitimate, safe, decent and plausible thing to do.

Here is some of what we might learn to tell ourselves in the face of our fears:

i. We are not revolting
We know, of course, how much there is that is unappealing and wrong about us. We are the masters of self-hatred; we know all our worst angles, every mistake we've ever made, every idiotic thing we've ever said. In certain moods, we cannot put any of this out of

our minds and so grow tongue-tied and furtive, fleeing any possibility of new connections. It feels as if we are wretched beings and that no one we admire could ever begin to care about us, let alone want to exchange a few pleasantries with us. But we are, of course, being monstrously harsh on ourselves; we are bringing a cruel and unwarranted perfectionism to bear on our characters. We are deeply flawed, but so, fortunately, is everyone else. Our errors and ugly sides do not cast us out from humanity, they are what join us to it – and render us all the more hungry for, and deserving of, love. We do not claim to be ideal, but nor is anyone else. We should, perhaps, dare to say hello without panicking at our shadow sides.

ii. A rejection won't have to be a rejection of the whole of us
What we are terrified of is not just a 'no' but everything that a 'no' ends up symbolising in our anxious minds:

a definitively negative verdict on the whole of our characters, a confirmation that we don't in essence deserve to be. It isn't a brush-off that is at stake; a rejection from another person threatens to confirm all our worst thoughts about ourselves. But the truth is that, if a refusal were to come, it would not have to be a plebiscite on our right to exist. It won't be that they loathe us profoundly or are sickened by our very existence, but rather that they are perhaps already with someone else, or are in need of some time by themselves after a harsh break-up, or have physical tastes that run quite innocently in a different direction. None of it needs to be taken as a profoundly personal rebuke. We should not let our own tendencies to self-hatred blend in with the inevitable accidents and mismatches of every journey through the dating world.

iii. People may be a lot less closed off than they seem

The desirable ones have a habit of appearing hugely self-contained and complete. They don't look as if they would be interested in meeting anyone new or as if they could have space in their lives for someone like us. They seem entirely content, reading their book on the promenade or chatting to their friends by the check-in desk. But there is often more space in others' hearts than the surface may suggest. We know from our own experience how much, despite an often busy and competent life, we maintain an appetite for novelty, for new kinds of interaction and sincerity, for fresh sources of kindness and interest. We know how open we might at points be to an approach from a self-aware and well-meaning stranger. This isn't because there is anything deficient in us but because it's the human norm to be somewhat dissatisfied with parts of one's existence and to be occasionally curious about how things might go with another person. It isn't impossible that someone we like the look of could, at the very same time as us, quietly harbour a hungry heart.

iv. We will soon be dead

It seems terrifying to try, of course, but in the broader scheme of our lives, the risk we are taking by saying hello does not deserve the terror we sometimes anxiously afford it. We can survive a no. We will soon enough be stone cold dead and should use the idea of our own (more or less) impending doom to make us less scared of the many petty challenges that stand in the way of our plans for happiness – before it is all too late. We should panic ourselves about one big thing so as to loosen our hold on our day-to-day inhibitions. The thing we must really be afraid of is not to hear that they already have a partner or pre-existing plans for lunch, but that we will reach the grave without having dared to try to say hello.

v. We are idiots, of course

We are terrified of coming across as foolish. But rather than harbouring this fear in a secret part of our fearful selves, we should make ourselves entirely at peace with our dread – and gain confidence from an open-hearted acceptance of our own and everyone else's clumsy ridiculousness. Of course we are idiots. If we stumbled and said a silly thing, it shouldn't ever be news to us, just confirmation of an already well-established and quite unshameful truth about everyone: that doing stupid things is a basic feature of being human. Though we can't possibly guess at the exact details, the person in front of us must also have done a great many ridiculous and strange things in their own lives. Being a bit of an idiot does not disqualify us from the possibility of love.

vi. They might have had a rather ugly parent

They, of course, look sublime, which may feel like

an argument for never daring to speak to them. We readily imagine that they could only love someone as perfectly formed as they are. But the laws of biology and psychology may work hugely in our favour in the background. We tend to fall in love with people who remind us of the parent of the gender we're attracted to – and, mercifully, many beautiful people had ugly parents. They may themselves look stunning, but their personal histories can mean that they will be inclined to look with deep benevolence on our own physical shortcomings, which may touchingly remind them of their beloved bald and short father or kind-hearted yet plain-looking mother.

vii. The most attractive people are often left alone
We imagine, naturally, that they will already have countless offers. Their wonderfulness immediately suggests as much and, out of modesty, we walk away.

The irony is that everyone will tend to think the very same thing and therefore, ironically, they may be far more neglected than less conspicuously special candidates. Beyond this, we make a more profound error. We forget how much turmoil, inner doubt and loneliness quite naturally accompany people's more visible qualities. A person may feel anxious and at sea despite a face that everyone is in awe of. Someone's gargantuan accomplishments at work may spring from, or be helpless to assuage, a latent feeling of being undeserving and shameful. The people we admire may still need our love.

None of these are lines we direct at another person; they are all things we can afford to say to ourselves as we try to do that most implausible and needlessly scary of things: introduce ourselves to an as yet unknown human we might one day share our lives with.

HOW TO PROVE ATTRACTIVE
TO SOMEONE ON A DATE

The goal can be stated simply enough: The overwhelming priority when on a date with someone we like is to persuade them to like us back.

But the simplicity of the mission masks the complexity required to achieve it. Typically, the advice focuses on externals: whether to take a jacket, when to unfurl a napkin, what to order ... But such counsel, however well-meaning, is at odds with what we ourselves know about attraction: that it is profoundly based on psychology.

However much we may deny it to friends, a date is ultimately a search for a potential long-term partner. So what really renders someone attractive on a date are signs that they are emotionally well-equipped for what a good-enough long-term relationship requires. The capacity to pick out an ideal full-bodied Chianti on a menu may be impressive, but what we're really primed to be stirred by are signs that someone is going to be a decent companion twenty years from now when we have received a difficult medical diagnosis or are feeling weepy and ashamed at the progress of our careers.

Here then are some of the things we might do to prove attractive to another person on a date:

i. *Tell them that we are a bit mad*

We might, in the course of the conversation, light-heartedly drop in that we're not quite sane. Perhaps we have great difficulty getting to sleep or get very anxious in social situations. Maybe we are often deeply sad on Sunday evenings or have a painful rivalry with a sibling.

The key is that, as we reveal these vulnerabilities, we can suggest that we have a mature, compassionate, unruffled relationship to them. Yes, we may be a little mad, but we are eminently sane enough to know about, and be unfrightened by, our follies; we have mapped them, are able to warn others of them and can protect those we love from their worst consequences. What we require in a partner is not someone who is perfect, but someone who has a good handle on their manifold imperfections.

It is deeply reassuring to witness vulnerability well-worn and madness confidently understood; to see someone mature enough to talk about their immaturities in a non-defensive and serene way.

Over the long term, every possible partner will be revealed as rather crazy in some dimension of existence or another. So what really counts is not whether or not someone is psychologically complicated, but how they relate to this complexity: the degree of insight, calm, perspective and humour they can bring to bear upon it.

Conversely, there should be nothing more terrifying on a date than a person who sticks a little too aggressively to the idea that they are totally sane and entirely normal. Anyone over the age of twenty possessed of the idea that they are 'easy to live with' has evidently not begun to understand themselves or their impact upon others. We should skip dessert and head home early.

ii. Ask our partners how they are a bit mad

The enquiry should sound playful, natural and wholly compassionate. Having laid out our flaws of character, we should take it as a given that – despite their strengths and accomplishments – our date too will have a litany of their own madder sides. We should imply that it is unsurprising that our date should be a bit 'broken' in certain areas; everyone is. We can gently enquire into what makes them particularly anxious or depressed, what was untenably difficult in their childhoods or what they regret and are ashamed of. This can prove charming because what we're ultimately looking for in love are not people who find us perfect, but people who will not flinch from our reality. We want to be seen for who we really are and forgiven for our flaws; not mistaken for someone else, idealised – and then one day accused of deceit.

iii. Reveal we've been a bit lonely and sad lately

We often assume that people want to hear that things are going brilliantly for us – and that we become winning for others when we can show we're triumphing in the world. But in truth, what really endears us to others is evidence that they share in some of the very difficulties and confusions that we are beset by at our core. If love involves a desire for an end to loneliness, then some of what we no longer want to be lonely with are our more melancholy dimensions that most people have no interest in – and that we therefore have to hide from them in a bid to look competent and strong.

How seductive, therefore, to stumble on someone around whom we sense we will no longer have to be jolly; someone who can give us room, through their own candour, to confess to feelings of loss and sorrow. There can be few things more charming on a date than to hear, from someone who looks extremely self-possessed and competent, that they've been feeling unusually isolated and very perplexed of late. They're showing us the fertilised soil in which mutually supportive love can grow.

iv. Pay some compliments

We can, understandably, get anxious at the idea of having to pay our date some compliments. The approach can feel too direct, demanding, almost sleazy. But there is an art to good compliments that starts from a different place: a recognition that most of us struggle to maintain a basic grasp on what is decent and good about us, and that we privately hunger to hear some basic, soothing, psychologically sustaining things about our characters (that sound unbelievable when we try to say them to ourselves): that we aren't wholly stupid, that some of the things we say have value, that we are sometimes funny or perceptive and that we have a few qualities to contribute to the world.

We can be so worried by our own inadequacies that we forget that the person across the table will have an equally large share of them – which it lies within our power to calm. With our date, we run few risks if we hint delicately at one or two of the reasons why we found them a decent person to invite out; we should not underestimate how deeply – in the quiet of their souls – everyone tends to be suspicious of themselves.

v. Blush

For anyone with a tendency to blush, the idea that there might be something positive about going uncontrollably red in front of another person on a date can sound absurd. But however uncomfortable it may be to blush, doing so indicates a range of admirable character traits we should honour in ourselves and welcome in others. Far from a disability, blushing is a sign of virtue. It's strong evidence that one is, almost certainly, rather a nice person. We tend to blush from a fear that something about us might bother or prove unacceptable to other people. We blush after we've told a joke and worry that it might have come across as inappropriate. We blush when we are concerned that something we said sounded boastful. We blush because we told a little untruth, feel ashamed and fear someone else might see through us. We blush that we may desire someone who doesn't feel the same way about us – and we absolutely don't want to bother them.

In other words, blushing is powered by a terror of making others uncomfortable or inconveniencing them, and a distaste for seeming arrogant or entitled.

Excessive self-doubt can, of course, blight our lives. But blushing seems to spring from an advanced self-awareness that would strongly keep any of our more unappealing sides in check over the long-term future we're auditioning for.

vi. Do something clumsy

We knock over a glass, drop some food down our front or jog the bread basket off the edge of the table. It feels like a disaster, but so long as we handle our own clumsiness with humour, and admit good-naturedly the scale of our own ineptitude, we can turn the situation to our advantage. We are signalling that we know that what matters isn't simply the errors we make but how we explain and frame them to those around us. Across a lifetime, we're going to do plenty of ridiculous things, so what counts is to be able to show at the earliest moment, as we mop up the mayonnaise or wipe a drop of tiramisu from a nearby oil painting, that we can handle adversities and reversals without fuss or drama; that we are modest and wise enough not to expect perfection from ourselves and will hence be able to forgive slip-ups and failure in others.

These and more belong to a properly rich sense of what we might need for the audition of our lives that we call, with touching modesty, a date.

WHAT TO TALK ABOUT

Our initial impulse might be to pick up on a current event, some detail of the environment or a few impressive things about our careers. But if a date is a test for the success of a long-term relationship, then what we should really be pursuing is mutual understanding of our deeper selves.

We know we will be doing well if, at a certain point, our date reflects that they've never been asked so many psychologically weighty questions, and asks if we are perhaps some sort of psychotherapist in training.

This is some of what we might ask as we try to take the measure of another's true identity:

What has made you cry in recent times?
We're not only concerned with what goes well for them; we're accepting of, and curious about, their reversals. We know that there are painful sides of life for everyone, and so we're not going to insist on levity or deny them the right to grieve. We'll also be sure to tell them in turn what brings tears to our eyes.

What was difficult in your childhood?
Without anyone meaning for this to happen, parents inevitably bruise and damage their children. With a light touch, we're trying to get a sense of their particular take on the drama of growing up. All of us end up a little distorted by our experiences: over-vigilant or too relaxed; too concerned with money or overly indifferent

to material goods; frightened of sex or excessively decadent. They won't be unique in having been messed up, we're clear on this score, but their disturbances will be fascinatingly specific to them. We're signalling that understanding their childhood self will be vital to grasping how they behave and who they are as adults.

What do you regret?

Our lives are crucially defined by the roads that weren't taken, by the choices we bungled, by the situations we ruminate on in the early hours. Because there is such a risk of humiliation in revealing where we messed up, if we can be patient and compassionate listeners, we will be doing something for our date that almost no one has ever done for them – at least outside of a professional therapeutic context. We will be gifting them the honour of feeling heard for sometimes being less than admirable, and of being reassured that this is just an inevitable feature of being human; it will be a luxury far greater than being taken to a lauded restaurant or rooftop bar.

To whom would you like to go back and apologise?
An associated enquiry, this one focuses on the guilt we accumulate as we stumble through our lives. It's a question that both leaves room for confession and offers atonement.

What would you want someone to forgive you for?
Gently, we're probing at what they know is tricky in their own characters. We aren't brutally asking what is wrong with them. We're inviting them to admit to one or two ways in which they have noticed that they can cause difficulties for others. We'll need to have some examples of our own follies to confess to straight after.

What have your exes not understood about you?

Past relationships are the repositories of clues as to the success of future ones. We're wondering how well they can pinpoint what went wrong and whether failure has provided them with an occasion to learn rather than merely lament or blame.

What would you ideally want to tell your mother?
And your father?

There might be tears at the thought. There can be so much buried sorrow in the history we share with the two people on earth we tend to love and hate in almost equal measure – and owe so much to. We will listen to what a set of parents were too brittle, too defensive or too proud to hear. It'll be everything that never comes out at family gatherings but that so urgently needs to be aired.

In what ways do you feel like a bit of an impostor at work?
We're normalising that we all invariably feel like we don't entirely measure up to what is expected of us professionally. We're providing a refuge for a sense of incompetence that we take such pains to hide from the world in normal circumstances. We're inviting the other, at last, to let down their guard.

Having exchanged these questions, and others like them, over many hours, we may feel something odd starting to happen: We may sense ourselves falling a little in love. The process isn't mysterious; it's just that we're getting to know one another's deeper selves, with all the longings, errors, terrors, regrets, weaknesses and fears involved. There is simply nothing more seductive than this kind of mutual self-revelation, love being in large part the gratitude we register when we feel accepted and seen – as well as the compassion we experience when another person lets down their defences and trusts that we will be kind to them for all that is imperfect and broken in them.

SUPPLEMENTARY EARLY DATE
CONVERSATION OPTIONS

Complete the following sentences:
> *If I were not so shy, I would ...*
> *If someone truly knew me, they would ...*
> *When I start to like someone, I worry that ...*

What kind of character trait that you don't possess do you find attractive in others?

What do you look for in a very close friend?

How did your childhood leave you less than ideally equipped for life?

Which of your friends do you envy the most?

What too often goes wrong in conversation?

SUPPLEMENTARY EARLY DATE
CONVERSATION OPTIONS

In what respects are you still the same person you were as a child?

What would you like to change about yourself?

In what ways is your family especially odd?

What are you prone to being addicted to?

What do you fear people might say about you behind your back?

List your top three worries in your life at the moment.

What has been the role of money in your family?

WHAT TO EAT & DRINK ON A DATE

Restaurants have traditionally enjoyed a crucial and privileged place in the history of dating, providing us with enough privacy to get to know one another and enough public scrutiny to help us feel safe as we do so. The meal has largely been an excuse.

But what we decide to eat and drink together isn't merely incidental to the real task of mutual understanding. It too is rich in psychological clues, communicating messages about who we are and what we might be like over a lifetime. How we order can, in a minor key, belong to the task of winning someone else over to our cause. Let's think of a number of ways of ordering food and drink that suggest intriguing and complex things about our identities:

What we might order:

A large mixed salad, accompanied by a plate of fries on the side. We could eat the fries with our fingers and occasionally dip them in the vinaigrette.

What we'd be communicating:

That we're pretty sensible in many ways, with a keen eye for restraint and a decent amount of self-control. But at the same time, that we aren't afraid of our own more impish desires. We're hinting that we are a sound blend of the mischievous and the prudent, and that we have enough self-mastery and obedience to feel we have the right to occasional moments of unorthodox indulgence.

What we might order:

Almost nothing.

What we'd be communicating:

After putting in our bare order, we might allow ourselves to say with beguiling frankness that we are simply too nervous to eat. This would be importantly different from – and much more attractive than – merely ordering a normal amount, then pushing it idly around our plate. We'd be showing that we were upfront in revealing that the date meant a lot to us, and that there was in our eyes nothing shameful about being anxious in relation to an event that might turn out to be hugely significant. Our inability to countenance any dessert whatsoever (not even a few berries) would be a flattering way of sending out a message that we were in the company of someone with the power to alter our lives.

What we might order:

Fish fingers off the children's menu.

What we'd be communicating:

Through our order, we're implying that we can recognise, without anxiety, the claim of the more childish parts of our personalities, but that we are sufficiently grown up to be undisturbed by their presence. The order might work best if we combine it with an obviously sophisticated starter or dessert. No one can be free of the legacy of their early past, we'd be saying through our food; what matters is the maturity with which we can acknowledge and navigate around it.

What we might order:

Cranberry juice.

What we'd be communicating:

The deep red drink would be a symbol of independence; we'd be making a rather unconventional order, this not being what people typically ask for in a restaurant. But it wouldn't be wilful or crazy either. We'd just be quietly asserting that we didn't mind appearing a little odd for the sake of getting something we genuinely liked. We'd be saying, via the glass, that we were our own sort of people.

What we might order:

The chicken, but – we'd add with a large smile and a hugely polite and patient explanation – ideally without the ginger and garlic, and with the sauce on the side in a little jug, and apologies to the chef, who we really hope wouldn't be put out by this sort of (in our words) 'unbearably fussy' request.

What we'd be communicating:

That we know our tastes are complicated and off the beaten track, but that we have the self-belief and requisite charm to lay out our desires calmly and without undue or grating petulance. Everyone in relationships turns out in time to harbour a host of very particular requirements; no one, however casual they might appear at first, is ever really 'easy' in the long term. So what matters hugely is if we have learnt the art of communicating our needs clearly, with grace, without entitlement or wilfulness, with the wit and will of the best teacher – an accomplishment we have a great chance to display in our approach to the ordering of the main course.

What we might eat:
Something we hadn't even ordered, but that was sitting on our date's plate and that looked especially appealing – and that we'd very sweetly ask if we could have a bit of.

What we'd be communicating:
That we are ready to step over conventional barriers in the name of friendship; that we understood there are certain standard obstacles to intimacy but that we are interested in finding a few playful ways of getting past them – possibly later that night.

WHAT TO WEAR

What we wear at points contains some of our most carefully chosen and eloquent lines of autobiography. Our clothes can tell the world a host of things about who we really are. When dressing for a date, the issue of what to wear is therefore particularly fraught: What message do we want to send? What little essay do we want to write about ourselves in the language of garments?

Ideally we should use clothes to suggest that we possess characteristics that are helpful to the success of long-term relationships. So before we even choose what to wear, we need to ask ourselves what qualities, which we actually possess, we might seek to foreground to a prospective partner.

A hopeful though unexpected guide here is the ancient Greek philosopher Aristotle. He noted that most humans tend to suffer from a range of excesses or deficiencies in their personalities, whereas the wise and mature among us possess qualities that sit in the middle between two opposing polarities: in what he called the golden mean of personality.

We can think about clothing as an opportunity to reveal a seductive Aristotelian balance in ourselves. We might seek to communicate inner balance by dressing in ways that happen to be both ...

Luxurious *and* thrifty

There are moments when the term 'luxury' stands for impressive craftsmanship, admirable attention to detail and due investment in quality – but an exclusive demand for it can also be a sign of an overly exigent and immature soul. On the other hand, thrift is an admirable quality – but a relentless preoccupation with paring down expenditure can be withholding, unimaginative and dispiriting.

What we're really seeking – and what we might personally have achieved – is a judicious balance between an appreciation of the charms of luxury and a wise and sane respect for the value of economy, the capacity to recognise that something can be very nice even though it might not cost very much. We can announce this kind of judicious balance through clothes by combining an inexpensive but pleasing garment with one obviously rather grand highlight, or by offsetting a rather fine piece of clothing with a conspicuously modest detail.

Childlike *and* mature

It's good, of course, to show that we're rather grown-up in our attitudes, but we risk an overly aloof relationship to the more playful, sweetly silly and childlike parts of who we are, which also constitute important strengths for coping with the challenges of life. Clothes can come to our aid in revealing to another person an attractive combination of gravity and whimsicality. To a sober and sensible base, we might add a rather naïve item. Our recognition of the claims of the one does not involve a denial of those of the other.

Our clothing is an eloquent advertisement for how we will be able to bring a broad set of emotional skills into different areas: in a discussion of finances, at a dinner party, at a school parents' evening, on the first day of the holidays.

Intellectual *and* sensuous

We are commonly at risk of either slipping into excessive and dry rationality or else falling prey to exaggerated emotional intensity. If our way of life is already outwardly rather intellectual, we might go out of our way to wear something unusually fashionable and up to the minute. If we normally come across as already pretty alive to the senses or as very lively, we might deliberately choose muted colours or shapes that allude to sober uniforms or practical workwear. In both cases, our intellectual vibrancy or sensual vivacity will come across anyway, but we'll be able to help our date to realise that there are other important aspects to who we are.

Conventional *and* original

Although being conventional can sound boring, it's clearly a major reassurance to others to note that we are capable of understanding and admiring the things that matter to most people ('conventional' just meaning 'in line with the attitudes of a significant majority'). But at the same time, it is also very reassuring to know that we're capable of putting aside the majority view at points and of being loyal to our own particular outlook and values. Through an adroit use of clothes, we can signal that we have found a path between two unfortunate extremes: the person who is always terrified of being thought odd and therefore stifles some interesting parts of who they are, and the person who is so worried about their individuality being ignored that they have to put themselves on a collision course with everything that is standard.

COMMON ODDITIES WE
MEET WHEN DATING

Dating exposes us to a far wider range of people than we generally encounter when we exist within the protection of a couple. It throws us into the wide sea of humanity and our encounters may lead us to a large and sobering conclusion: that human beings can be really very strange. Characters who might be plausible as mere acquaintances or office colleagues can reveal peculiarities normally concealed in ordinary social life. We're not only unlucky if our dates initiate us like this. We should accept that there are simply many fascinating things that can go wrong with the human spirit. If we're going to keep on dating, we have to take on board with a degree of good humour and open-hearted curiosity the fact that we will often be conducting incidental psychological experiments in the distortions that can occur to the psyche. Rather than complain about how awful most of our dates turn out to be, we should get interested in understanding – and even sympathising with – the varieties of human brokenness.

The name-dropper
They're always finding ways to let you know who they know and who they've met. Their uncle once employed someone who worked for the Queen; their work sent them to a hotel where Tom Cruise stayed; recently there was an heir to a banking fortune on their plane. They don't even notice they're doing it. It is, of course, quite off-putting, but we should be tender to the reasons why it's happening. It seems as if they might have ended up

boasting and grandstanding because they're so pleased with themselves. Far from it. Boasting is only ever a response to feeling invisible. We so badly need to thrust forward an idea of our own importance because (behind the scenes) our very right to exist is something we are very far from convinced of. We see it as almost inevitable that others will think ill of us – unless we urgently and dramatically assert our connections with greatness. That is why, of all people, name-droppers don't need to be told they are terrible. That's precisely what they secretly think already. They need encouragement to feel a more genuine pride in their own merits, so as not to feel such an impulse to lean on the names of others.

The overly cheerful

A type often encountered in the dating realm, the overly cheerful person is not happy because external reasons justify the mood; they are determined to look exclusively on the bright side because anything sadder or more realistic is unbearable to them. We can't precisely see the large threat they feel they are warding off, but there will almost certainly be something in the past which has made them poignantly unable to look with resilience upon the negative aspects of existence. Perhaps there was a furious, disturbed parent who would explode if things weren't perfect and sunny, or a depressed parent who could be profoundly incapacitated by a small disappointment. To survive such challenges, our date acquired a habit of presenting a relentlessly jolly face to the world. It makes the evening something of a trial, for we can sense how much of reality and of our own lives will be unacceptable to them, but we can still feel very sorry for them for the events that made their jolly censorship feel so necessary.

The overly intellectual

They want to let us know all that they have been reading and the big ideas currently animating the worlds of science and philosophy, government and tech. They want to fill our minds with impressive ideas, which blatantly announce their intelligence to the world. To be simple and straightforward is – for precise reasons we won't be able to get hold of but which we can easily enough imagine in their broad outlines – to risk humiliation. To say they don't know or don't understand, to admit to being confused, ignorant or uninformed are unbearable possibilities. They might have been shouted at for their ignorance in childhood. They might have been the victims of early humiliation against which big ideas seem to offer a defence. Perhaps they deploy knowledge and concepts that carry vast prestige to stand guard against the emergence of more humble but essential knowledge from their emotional past.

They bury their personal stories beneath an avalanche of expertise. We might have wanted to get to know them, but they are, it seems, at heart too traumatised to be able to offer us very much more than the latest ideas from the *New York Review of Books* and the *New England Journal of Medicine*.

The under-intellectual

Then there are people we meet who insist that they are simpler than they really are and that too much psychology might be nonsense and fuss about nothing. They lean on a version of robust common sense, perhaps to ward off intimations of their own awkward complexity. They imply that not thinking very much is, at base, evidence of a superior kind of intelligence. They deploy bluff strategies of ridicule against more complex accounts of human nature. They sideline avenues of personal investigation as unduly fancy or weird, implying that to lift the lid on inner life could never be fruitful or entirely respectable. They can be very trying.

The ranters

The more we date, the higher the risk that one evening we will end up trapped with a person of excessive conviction or, to put it more colloquially, a bore who rants. Such types can be found harbouring any manner of obsessions: They may be deeply concerned about grammar (and the ever-increasing misuse of the subjunctive); they may be horrified by the predatory nature of contemporary capitalism or disgusted by the whingeing of the environmental movement; they might hate feminism or see misogyny in every corner of life. Bores aren't necessarily wholly misguided – they may be making some very good points along the way – but our discomfort in their company arises from the intensity and relentlessness of their manner. Bores bore because we sense that they are not being entirely honest with us. They are certainly upset, but the real reasons why don't seem on offer. We feel – in the midst of their explanations – that their intensity is drawing heat from a source beyond the argument as they define it. They may well be emphasising a range of studiously impersonal political, economic or social factors, but we intuit that there must be a more personal story from which we, and their conscious selves, are being carefully shielded.

When we come across their ardent views, it isn't that we want to hear less; it's rather that we would ideally want to hear more, but in another direction, inwards rather than further into sociocultural and economic abstractions. And we want to do this not from prurience but because dating life is guided by a wish to encounter the reality of other people – which is here being arcanely denied. Our boredom is at base an impatient resentment at being held at bay from the genuine traumas of another's life.

People who believe in being cool
Cool people on dates can sound, on the surface, like a very nice idea. They don't seem overly pleased to see us and that can, in certain moods, be almost thrilling. They don't try too hard; they express themselves only briefly. If the house were on fire, the cool date wouldn't scream or call the fire brigade; 'temperature's rising' they might quip, then casually put out the blaze themselves. Were the waiter to spill a cocktail over them, they wouldn't get flustered; they would remove their jacket and look even better without it.

But coolness can have its tedious and oppressive sides. How would it be possible to be vulnerable around such an impermeable being? How could they understand what scares or excites us? We might sense that beneath their coolness was an impression that it was dangerous to ever show much enthusiasm, as if they were worried that if they appeared naïve or sensitive, they would be appallingly humiliated and rejected. Perhaps they had to ditch their childhood selves too early. At a key moment they might have felt in real danger if they ever expressed an opinion or preference that didn't coincide with the cynical attitudes of the 'in' group. They weren't granted a sense that they could be safe and loved and interesting even if they listened to the 'wrong' music or said something silly, touching, sad or childlike. There won't be much for our affection to hold on to.

WHY THE FIRST KISS MAY
BE THE BEST SEX WE EVER HAVE

The crowning achievement of a successful date is normally one of the strangest acts of which two humans are capable. One moment we are exchanging smiles, looking a bit too long into each other's eyes and talking about not very much. The next, we lean in towards them and they to us, we tilt our heads just a little, then we feel their mouth opening slightly and the tip of their tongue sliding past our teeth. Two organs otherwise used for eating and speaking are rubbed and pressed against one another with increasing force, accompanied by the secretion of saliva. A tongue normally precisely manipulated to articulate vowel sounds, or to push mashed potato or broccoli to the rear of the palate, moves forward to meet its counterpart, whose tip it might touch in repeated staccato movements. One would have to explain carefully to an alien visitor from Kepler-9b what is going on. We are not about to bite chunks out of each other's cheeks, or attempting to inflate the other person.

Why is kissing so significant and potentially so exciting? Why is this how a good date is meant to end? The excitement is at heart psychological. It's not so much what our mouths happen to be doing that is satisfying; it's what's happening in our imaginations that matters.

The excitement of kissing is the result of social codes being breached. We could imagine a society where it was very forbidden, and yet very special, for two people to rub the gap between the index finger and thumb together. The first time you did it would be something you'd remember all your life. The huge meaning of kissing is something we've built up by social agreement and its fundamental definition is: I accept you – enough to do something potentially quite revolting with you.

The inside of a mouth is deeply private. Ordinarily it would be utterly nauseating to have a stranger poke their tongue into your face. To allow someone to do these things signals a fundamental level of acceptance.

All of us suffer from strong feelings of shame, which another's kiss starts to work on overcoming. Eroticism is the pleasure – in which relief plays a big part – at having our secret sexual selves witnessed, endorsed and encouraged by a kindly other.

There's an assumption at large that sexiness must at heart be about nakedness and explicitness – and that logically, therefore, the sexiest scenarios must also be the ones involving the greatest amounts of nudity. But the truth about excitement is rather different. At the core of sexiness is an idea: the idea of being allowed into someone's life, when the memory of having been excluded from it is at its most vivid. Sexiness stems from the contrast between prohibition and acceptance. It is a species of relief and thanks at being given permission to belong with someone else.

This gratitude is likely to be most prevalent not when one has been granted full licence by someone, but when one is on the borderline, when one has only just been lent a pass – and when the memory of the taboo of touching others is still intense: in other words, on an early successful date. The reminder of the danger of rejection brings the wonder at being included into sharp, ecstatic relief.

Later on, if the relationship develops and grows, we might stop appreciating how extraordinary it is that our date once let us into their lives. We might find nothing surprising at all about seeing them cross the room naked. We should try out a few games to remember to appreciate our intimacy a little more. We might want to keep our clothes on a bit longer than strictly necessary. To heighten excitement, we might design a scenario in which we were only 'allowed' to press against one another, never moving beyond guilty caresses and small thrusts – as though we were on an early date ...

Such games mean we can keep revisiting the incredible idea of mutual permission that manifests itself most clearly at the start. If a date goes well, we'll certainly have a lot more sex than we had the night we first kissed, but it might never be quite as moving and erotic as that first brush of the lips.

SHOULD WE PLAY IT COOL
WHEN WE LIKE SOMEONE?

One of the paradoxes of the dating game is that we know that by coming across as enthusiastic at an early stage – if we ring them the next day, if we are open about how attractive we find them, if we suggest meeting them again very soon – we are putting ourselves at a high risk of disgusting the very person we would so like to build a relationship with.

It is in order to counter this risk that, early on in our dating lives, we are taught by well-meaning friends to adopt a facade of indifference. We become experts at deliberately not phoning or sending messages, at treating our dates in a carefully off-hand manner and in subtly pretending that we don't much care if we never cross their paths again. We are told that the only way to get them to care about us is to pretend not to care for them. And in the process, we waste a lot of time, we may lose them altogether and we have to suffer the indignity of denying that we feel a desire that should never have been associated with shame in the first place.

But we can find a way out of the conundrum by drilling deeper into the philosophy that underpins the well-flagged danger of being overly eager. Why is detachment so often recommended? Why are we not meant to call too soon?

High levels of enthusiasm are generally not recommended for one central reason: because they have been equated with what is a true psychological problem: manic dependence. In other words, calling too soon has become a symbol of weakness, desperation and the inability to deal adequately with life's challenges without the constant support of a lover, whose real identity the manically keen party doesn't much care about, because their underlying priority is to ensure that they are never alone without someone, rather than with any one being in particular.

We should, however, note that what is ultimately the problem is manic dependence, not high enthusiasm. The difficulty is that our cultural narratives have unfairly glued these two elements together with an unnecessarily strong and unbudging kind of adhesive.

Yet there should logically be an option to disentangle the two strands – that is, to be able to reveal high enthusiasm and, at the same time, not thereby to imply manic dependence. There should be an option to appear at once very keen and very sane.

The ability to do so depends on a little known emotional art to which we seldom have recourse or introduction: strong vulnerability. The strongly vulnerable person is a diplomat of the emotions who manages carefully to unite on the one hand self-confidence and independence, and on the other a capacity for closeness, self-revelation and honesty. It is a balancing act. The strongly vulnerable know how to confess with authority to a sense of feeling small. They can sound in control even while revealing that they have an impression of being lost. They can talk as adults about their childlike dimensions. They can be unfrightening at the same time as admitting to their own fears. And they can tell us of their immense desire for us while simultaneously leaving us under the impression that they could fully survive a frank rejection. They would love to build a life with us, they imply, but they could very quickly and adroitly find something else to do if that didn't sound like fun from our side.

In the way that the strongly vulnerable speak of their desire for us, we sense a beguiling mixture of candour and independence. They don't need to play it cool because they carry off high enthusiasm in a way which sidesteps the dangers it has traditionally and nefariously been associated with.

What is off-putting is never in fact that someone likes us; what is frightening is that they seem in danger of having no options other than us, of not being able to survive without us. Manic dependence, not enthusiasm, is only ever the problem. With this distinction in mind, we should learn to tell those we like that we're really extremely keen to see them again, perhaps as early as tomorrow night, and find them exceptionally marvellous – while simultaneously leaving them in no doubt that we could, if the answer were a no, without trouble and at high speed, find some equally enchanting people to play with and be bewitched by.

TWO REASONS WHY
WE MAY BE SINGLE

The common-sense explanation for long-term singlehood directs the blame firmly outwards. It isolates the problem to one of mechanics: One is still single because one hasn't, perhaps on account of having moved to a vast and anonymous new city, been invited to enough parties, or because the constant requirement to fly to the Singapore office leaves no time for the right sort of socialising, or because one is holed up in a remote village high in the mountains, connected to the more densely populated lowlands only by an irregular bus service.

These may be solid enough reasons, but when the problems persist over an extended period, their power to explain our situation weakens. Without anything remotely persecutory or unkind being intended by this, one is forced to cast around for psychological rather than procedural explanations. The problem must lie in our minds rather than in the world. And in the recesses of these minds, two issues – diametrical yet complementary – can often be identified: One is suffering from an excess of self-hatred, or from an excess of self-love.

Self-hatred is the more poignant of the pair. On being approached by someone, however initially attractive and competent they might be, we begin to wonder why they should be so naïve, so desperate and so weak as to be drawn to us. When we are inadequately convinced of our own likeability, the attentions of another person must forever seem illegitimate and peculiar, and reflect poorly on their donor. Love feels like a gift we haven't earned, don't deserve and must therefore take care eventually to throw away. We might, under the pressure of self-hatred, accuse our admirer of naïvety. The only possible reason they can have to approve of us is that they are poor judges of character. That is why they have missed all the more disturbed and darker aspects of us. They like us only because they are blind – and therefore a little stupid. However, because they are bound to spot their error eventually, it is surely wiser to run away before we are exposed and abandoned.

We end up alone because, despite our longing for affection, we don't in essence feel there are any good and lasting reasons why anyone would properly see us as we really are and like us. We may also, in the face of the gifts, text messages or hugs we receive, start to feel that our admirer is, to a sickening degree, needy. We feel repulsed by their need when we don't see ourselves as appropriate targets of anyone's need; we reject their nascent dependence because, somewhere inside, we are sure that we are not people to depend upon.

And yet, of course, none of these spectres need to be real in the world outside our touchingly troubled minds. The person who is keen on us is almost certainly not naïve. They can no doubt see us for what we are; they have noticed many of our less admirable sides. It is just that they don't consider these fatal, because they know that being not quite right is what all of us are and is no barrier to a mature relationship. They know we're not exactly who we think we should be, but they also grasp that this doesn't place anyone in the category of the damned. We might be a bit perverted, a little silly and not as nice as we make out – but so is everyone else. It's not that they are naïve about us; we're ultimately naïve about them. They know that every human has shadow sides. They've made peace with theirs (probably as a result of a fortunate childhood); they would like us to make peace with ours. Ahead of us, they understand that a person can be ordinarily imperfect – and worthy of being cherished.

Then, at the other end of the spectrum, comes excessive self-love, which really means a hesitation around fully acknowledging what a challenging proposition one is – and therefore how much we should rightly be grateful when someone, anyone with an ordinary share of strengths and weaknesses, looks our way.

Perhaps because of the legacy of doting and forgivably biased parents, we are operating with an unhelpful sense of how lucky someone might be to end up in our arms. After having been alone for a long time, we may also have lost the knack of spotting what peculiar, demanding and compulsive people we are. With no one to hold up a mirror, we have forgotten to give due weight to the rage, the anxiety and the moments of vindictiveness. At the same time, we are travelling the world with our imaginations switched off – imagination defined here as the capacity to look with energy, compassion and curiosity into the face and character of another person in order to search out what might be desirable and good therein.

Imagination means sensitivity to the less obvious things; one scans past the surface and wonders about what might be worthy inside a fellow human, whom it would – of course – always be so easy (yet ultimately so unrewarding) to criticise. To awaken the dormant faculty of the imagination, we might more regularly –

perhaps in the street or on the train to work – look at the faces around us, especially the less distinguished or obviously sculpted ones, and ask ourselves what there could be to delight in. There is always going to be something, for we were all once love-worthy children and remain as much in our depths.

Practising imagination is not a compromise, it is the key to love, for we all have to be considered imaginatively in order to be tolerated and forgiven over the long term by anyone. By thinking imaginatively, we're not being disloyal to the true ambition of love; we're stumbling on the essence of what love rightly has to involve. There will always be practical reasons why it proves hard to find a partner, but if we have worked on our levels of self-love and attenuated the ravages of self-hatred, an absence of parties or a difficult bus ride need never condemn us long term to a life devoid of tenderness and connection.

DATING TOO MUCH

Dating is generally conceived of as a search for another person with whom we can enjoy a long-term monogamous relationship; that is, logically speaking, the objective of dating is to stop dating.

But there are some of us who seem never to reach a point where dating can stop. Although we encounter dozens of people who could in varied ways be acceptable, we do not find anyone who exhausts our imagination and with whom we firmly want to retire from the dating game.

Romanticism offers us a beguiling explanation for this endless cycle: We simply haven't found The One, the exceptional person who truly deserves our long-term concern.

But we might adopt a slightly different way of thinking about what a good enough person to love might be by following an approach implicitly championed by one of dating's less obvious heroes, the 19th-century French painter Paul Cézanne, who over a decade towards the end of his life made a series of paintings of apples, which are widely counted as among the most charming works of art ever made. We may not despise the look of apples, but nor do we usually find them particularly exotic or exciting to observe. Cézanne did something very different. He spent years looking very carefully at a selection of apples and turned each one into a small globe of wonder. He would note the distinctiveness

Paul Cézanne, *Two Apples on a Table*, c. 1895–1900

of the colours; he would spot that in one there was a little more yellow than usual, and in another there was a fascinating reddish tinge on one side. He'd note the texture of the skins and trace every indentation and mark. He'd carefully observe the play of light and shadow over a curved surface and the precise angle of a stalk or leaf. Where we would most likely see just another average apple, Cézanne discovered an arresting object invested with a rich individual identity.

Some of what Cézanne achieved when painting apples applies obliquely to dating, for what is at stake in both cases is the generosity of the vision we can bring to bear on the world. The qualities we find in another person depend to a critical extent on the kind of curiosity and imagination we are able to summon. In a certain mood, everyone we meet can be dismissed as dull, routine, flawed and worthy of being passed over in an ongoing search for obvious glory. But in a different frame of mind, one of heightened sensitivity, many so-called average people can be revealed as repositories of immense value and fascination – and eminently deserving of love. What makes a person 'special' isn't in the end simply who they 'are', conceived of in some objective, unchanging way; it is the emotional complexity with which we know how to engage with them.

How long we keep dating for isn't therefore simply a matter of how long we must wait until we land upon an unambiguously exceptional person; it's also a question of how capable we are of searching out what is precious and worthy of love within the sort of people who regularly cross our paths.

Some of us keep dating forever not because we never meet someone who could deserve our attention but because we have not yet learnt the art of appreciation. We notice only the most overt problems, while leaving to one side the qualities that co-exist with them in the shadows. We don't discover that, perhaps, our date has a very sweet relationship with a younger sibling, or that over the years they have coped very well with a difficult parent; we don't find out that they've got an excellent way of dealing with conflict at work or are highly imaginative in the way they behave with children; we might not latch onto their ability to deal well with a setback or to set a distant goal and work patiently towards it.

In other words, we might already have met plenty of people who are profoundly worthy of our love. But in our rapid and dismissive glances, we haven't yet noticed the opportunity, much like so many of us hadn't spotted very much about ripe apples that was worth cherishing, until Cézanne took care to open our eyes.

One of the most important principles for choosing a lover sensibly is not to feel in any hurry to make a choice. Being satisfied with being single is a precondition of satisfactory coupledom. We cannot choose wisely when remaining single feels unbearable. We have to be utterly at peace with the prospect of solitude in order to have any chance of forming a good relationship, or we'll love no longer being single rather more than we love the partner who spared us being so.

Unfortunately, after a certain age, society makes

singlehood feel dangerously unpleasant. Communal life starts to wither. People in couples are too threatened by the independence of the single to invite them around very often, in case they are reminded of something they might have missed. Friendship and sex are, despite all the advances in technology, remarkably hard to come by. No wonder if when someone slightly decent, but not quite so, comes along, we cling to them, to our eventual enormous cost.

When sex was only available within marriage, people recognised that this led people to marry for the wrong reasons: to obtain something that was artificially restricted in society as a whole. Sexual liberation was intended to allow people to have a clearer head when choosing who they really wanted to be with. But the process remains only half-finished. Only when we make sure that being single can be potentially as secure, warm and fulfilling as being in a couple will we know that people are choosing to pair up for the right reasons. It's time to liberate 'companionship' from the shackles of coupledom, and make it as widely and as easily available as sexual liberators wanted sex to be.

In the meantime, we should strive to make ourselves as much at peace as we can with the idea of being alone for a very long time. Only then do we stand a chance of deciding to be with someone on the basis of their own true merits.

The difficulty of dating is the price we're quietly paying for eventually avoiding divorce.

WHAT WE WILL MISS ABOUT
OUR DATING YEARS

While we date, we generally hope that – one day soon enough – we won't have to keep doing this. Each new date might, if we're lucky, be the last one; the point at which the tension, the aggravation, the disappointment and the boredom can stop; the moment when we find someone whom we can at last write into our wills and with whom one evening, in thirty-five years' time, we will be able to babysit our first grandchild.

But if we succeed at dating, a strange thing can happen.

Over the decades of a long relationship, we may start to look back with a degree of tenderness and nostalgia on the dating period.

Of course there was pain. There were moments of terrible loneliness and humiliation; there were people we very much liked who never called back. There were evenings of comedically diverging tastes. There were people we met for dinner who should probably have been sent to a psychiatric institution instead.

But there was also glory and thrill to those dating years. We lived in a world of open possibilities: Any day could bring about a revolution in our feelings. We were meeting one to one with a remarkable selection of representatives of human nature: people who summed up the quirks and oddities of the species. For two or three hours or a few days, they let us glimpse the world through their eyes. They took us to places we'd otherwise never have gone to. We were introduced to an original way of spending an evening or to a distinctive idea of what breakfast might be. We found ourselves having conversations about immensely divergent things: the banking laws of Paraguay, the principle of organic farming, what it's like to have a parent in government or in prison. Life was open to us. We'd sample odd sexual situations, wake up in an apartment in an unfamiliar part of town, have showers in peculiar bathrooms, hear of strange relatives and family members – and feel ourselves born anew by being seen through fresh eyes.

And the deep irony, which we didn't appreciate at the time, is that though we thought we were failing at one thing, we were all along succeeding at another. Not having one special person kept us open and raw; not having made any choice gave colour and authenticity to our uncertain lives. In the end, we perhaps made a very good choice. But we lost a lot nevertheless.

It is so natural to want our dating days to come to an end, but we should never lose sight of the genuine merits and delights that lie closely entwined with their pains. We should continue to seek our life partner, while not ignoring the real pleasures that emerge from not yet having found them.

THE LOVE SERIES

There is no more joyful or troublesome area of our lives than love. From adolescence onwards, it is rare to go for any sustained length of time without some sort of fascinating or devilish new problem emerging around relationships.

The Love Series by The School of Life aims to be like an ideal friend around the dilemmas of the heart. Each title zeroes in on one of the central issues we're liable to confront – from dating to heartbreak, from affairs to arguments. What unites the books is their combination of psychological insight, humanity and warmth: They lend us the advice and comfort we need to find the happiness we deserve.